What Do You Want to See?

Seed Learning

What do you want to see?

A giraffe.

I want to see
a giraffe.

What do you want to see?

A penguin.

I want to see
a penguin.

What do you want to see?

A snake.

I want to see
a snake.

What do you want to see?

A panda.

I want to see
a panda.

What do you want to see?

A flamingo.

I want to see
a flamingo.

What do you want to see?

A hippo.

I want to see
a hippo.

What do you want to see?

A camel.

I want to see
a camel.

Let's learn more about Easter.

Color the egg.